WOLF HOWL

ALSO BY FRANCIS BLESSINGTON

POETRY
Lantskip

VERSE PLAY
Lorenzo de' Medici

VERSE TRANSLATIONS
Euripides: The Bacchae
Aristophanes: The Frogs

LITERARY CRITICISM
Paradise Lost and the Classical Epic
Paradise Lost: Ideal and Tragic Epic
The Motive for Metaphor (ed. with Guy Rotella)

WOLF HOWL

FRANCIS BLESSINGTON

Francis Blessington

BkMk Press
THE UNIVERSITY OF MISSOURI-KANSAS CITY

Copyright © 2000 by Francis C. Blessington. All rights reserved.

BkMk Press
University of Missouri-Kansas City
5100 Rockhill Road
Kansas City, Missouri 64110
(816) 235-2558
bkmk@umkc.edu

Financial assistance for this book has been provided by the Missouri Arts Council, a state agency.

Book design by Roxanne Witt
Cover design by Steve Duffendack

Library of Congress Cataloging-in-Publication Data

Blessington, Francis C., 1942-
    Wolf howl/Francis Blessington.
       p. cm.
    ISBN 1-886157-29-4
      I.   Title.

P3552.L443 W65 2000
811'.54—dc21
                            00-029738

10   9   8   7   6   5   4   3   2   1

Printed by Technical Communication Services, North Kansas City, Mo.

ACKNOWLEDGMENTS

Encouraging help came from Seamus Heaney, the late Samuel French Morse, Guy Rotella, and, my wife, Ann Taylor.

I would like to thank the editors of the following publications for publishing these poems, sometimes in slightly different versions:

Aileron, "First Step at Scilla" and "Sailing to the Isle of Man"; *Appalachia*, "Climber"; *The Christian Science Monitor*, "Sanding the Floor" and "Skating Again"; *Cumberland Poetry Review*, "Boustrophedon," "Coal Mine Museum", "Donkeys" and "Self-Portrait as Bored Boy"; *The Dalhousie Review*, "Anecdote of a Novelist" and "The Ascent of Snowdon"; *Descant*, "Desert Ruins" and "The Quarrel"; *Dialogos*, "Greek Shadow Puppet"; *Four Quarters*, "The Cellar"; *Frank*, "Three"; *Harvard Magazine*, "Father Smoking" and "On Looking into Chapman"; *National Forum*, "Wolf Howl"; *Off Main Street*, "Bells Off Salvador"; *The Pale Fire Review*, "Fern"; *Pegasus*, "They Call It 'The Wayfaring Tree'"; *Poet*, "In Bombay"; *Potpourri*, "Studio Nude"; *Puckerbrush Review*, "Afloat in Dogtown Moraine"; *Random Weirdness*, "Nocturne"; *The Sewanee Review*, "Changelings," "Firework," "Icework," and "Jungle Boy: Folk Artist"; *The Shakespeare Newsletter*, "The Wings"; *The South Florida Poetry Review*, "Everglades"; *The Southern Review*, "Caribou" and "Forms in Contemporary Poetry"; *Spectrum*, "Roost" and "Paradise Lost"; *Stone Country*, "The Man With the Umbrella"; *Thinker Review*, "Chinese Gallery"; *Wascana Review*, "English Fields"; *Yankee*, "Rehearsal: Eclipse of the Sun."

for Guy Rotella

CONTENTS

I

Skating Again   3
The Man With the Umbrella   5
Bells Off Salvador   6
First Step at Scilla   7
Three   8
Mothball Museum   9
The Wings   11
Apprenticeship:
      1. Roost   13
      2. Sanding the Floor   14
      3. Father Smoking   15
      4. The Cellar   16
Self-Portrait as Bored Boy   17
The Quarrel   18

II

Everglades   21
Studio Nude   24
English Fields   25
Nocturne   26

The Ascent of Snowdon   27
They Call It "The Wayfaring Tree"   29
Forms in Contemporary Poetry   30
In Bombay   31

III

Changelings   35
On Looking into Chapman   36
Knees   38
Two Greek Sketchings:
      1. Donkeys   39
      2. Greek Shadow Puppet   40
Paradise Lost   41
Boustrophedon   42
Anecdote of a Novelist   43
Jungle Boy: Folk Artist   45
Coal Mine Museum   46
Chinese Gallery   47

IV

Wolf Howl   51
Fern   53
Sailing to the Isle of Man   54

Climber 55

Caribou 56

Icework 58

Firework 59

Rehearsal: Eclipse of the Sun 60

Desert Ruins 61

Afloat in Dogtown Moraine 62

Notes 67

A Note on the Author 69

. . . at first a cry or a cadence or a mood and then a fluid and lambent narrative, finally refines itself out of existence, impersonalizes itself . . .

—James Joyce

I

Skating Again

Round and round again the shoveled plot,
Looping infinite eights,
Feeling that nothing is lost in a score of years,

I dazzle my son. He bows his knees like a sailor
To get his ice legs.
I haul him only a moment on his keel of gravity

Before he pratfalls gasping, roiling in snow foam
Outside the edge,
His double runners flopping lobsters.

The solid lake grunts and fissures
Its quarry of ice.
One belt links shore and shore.

Once my leg crashed to the hip and iced
Up for hours
As I rushed the goalie all day in stiff pride.

So now I dodge his hands; skateless he chases
On the slickness—
A blind man's buff of rebellious feet.

Two boys snap a puck; I wince
To see him play
With an ice block and my skate guard.

I turn wilder; when I stop my iron cuts,
Showers him with chips.
The surface groans louder.

He reclamps skates. Clenching teeth,
He wobbles ahead,
His mind upon the object, not this spectator.

Then he rights his angle like a mast.
That's it, darling,
Your ballast is true. You are sailing now—

Without this hand.

The Man with the Umbrella

His fishing lines rot in the cellar,
but he does not throw gear away,
since he treasures boyhood days in a dory.
On days of rain he lets the rain
soak his ashy face. With an umbrella
he fights off the sun's magnificence.

He sidles like a bat across storefronts,
ignorant of the heroism of birds,
the pigeon-swoop gleaning from the curb.
He feels the highway is greatly exaggerated,
pretends not to notice the odor of women,
and dodges the multiform faces we greet.

He is at home only in the Chinese Gallery,
where he breathes the dust from carved stone.
He has become the breath of worked stone
and the damp full somnambulance
of the cloud that covers up the skylight,
that repeats the memory of each dark shade.

Bells Off Salvador

Below our plane, a Mayan sunset gilds
and reddens the earthenware hills.
Our shadow, a small crucifix, thrums
and lands, like an unbrushed fly
upon a face rifle-butted near oblivion.
La matanza, la problema, los desaparecidos.

The silent curfew tolls. Light
blurts under a door after blackout
—like their paintings, the brush abstract,
phantasmagoric pastels chose partners; strafes dint
black across the canvas like crumpled monuments—
the poetry of San Juan de la Cruz.

A woman with unyielding square jaw
is rinsing a naked girl in a bucket shower.
She hands me an infant out a bureau drawer.
—At the dump, drilled holes in the corpses' teeth gaped.—
Outside, a carnation tree hangs its idle anthers.
My Miami ticket reads MIA.—

"Things missed off shelves: milk-powder,
Donnatol, people—a country smaller
than your state—no? Your binoculars
I try get back. Carry no money. Soldiers rob.
Feed him oranges, teach. Now, go.
Some year maybe, you make a photo."

First Step at Scilla

The beach is without center.
Waves streaming your gentle
crawl make you grip
my hand like a tow rope.
But the withdrawing roar
for you holds no fear.
You fix your feet
and make Charybdis' steep
swirl of salt water.
Then turn to Scylla's cliff in laughter
at standing the sea around
that no shame or gravity pulls you down.

Three

I heard retreating runs of shale
down the beach as I pooled the spilling
into my moat, and cousin clanked her pail.

I scooped clay with a suck of vowels.
With bright clam chips I inlaid something,
while the living gaped in the puddles.

Like a black-and-white photo,
beneath the boardwalk's seasoned graying,
a ghost barred by the salt-glare stood

and waved and laughed us back before
the seventh roiled us, shovels sprawling.
Around our ruddled figures: the tender

prints of gulls in the intertidal,
caws mingled with the gushing,
the snap of canvas, the mournful bottles:

the many mouths roaring, "ARE YOU COMING?"

Mothball Museum

The battleship's plumbing misleads us
among dry spigots and wheels.
A manikin sleeps in sick bay
under a "bloodied" cloth.

Lost as in hospital backrooms,
we pry the sealed hatches.
Flesh-painted walls mirror
no time, no direction, no help.

My son vaunts to his sister:
"Are we in Old Blood and Guts?"
He swings the iron, hollering
to future buddies through stairwells.

I relax my daughter on a kamikaze miniboat.
The bunks are empty shelves,
though one, glassed-in, is made-up.
I shout: "MacArthur said he'd be back."

Down the hall, the landlady's darkened room
kept us kids from Japanese dress swords;
till we broke in and roused our souls
with helmets and belling ears.

An open door. On deck I slip up the icy rungs
to possess a turret. My son aims
a stuffed fifteen incher at innocent gulls who bomb
the warship's sooted snow with white.

My daughter kills my son,
as if they had stayed unadopted in Salvador.
No one comes. And not one gull falls.
We are in command. Our anchor chains have lifted.

The Wings

(Shakespeare, *The Comedy of Errors*)

My son fumbles locked doors of sexual license
in wartime Ephesus amid an execution,
cut off in the nick, and a nymphetine
coed courtesan.

              Exorcism, adultery,
sword-play, children displaced
to teasing Mid-East gardens—megahertz beyond
the video's hidden princess and joystick sound-blastered flick
deaths.

              Hot flesh stalks his stage and death-wielding
monastic jokes. At leisure to pun obscenely,
he laughs at all baldpate, attendant fathers.
His strut widens wit to deliberate Courtier
insult.

              The voice plummets. His eyes
flutter mine to bankrupt virtue. Watch
him flash a hand and poltergeist
his masters

              —till the untying curtains all liberties.
and he joins with brother/sister/transvestite/slave
at the ducal palace for cash and wine
and prejudiced applause.

                              Stripped of buff,
he spasms stairs. In the backseat, he racks
his knuckles, trumpets fingers, and clenches to go on
becoming all that he does not know.

Apprenticeship

1. Roost

Crouched like a crow
My father drove nails
Either hand,
Wore a Sunday suit
Of rough-combed
Wool, even
On the roofs of summer.

Eyeing a bat behind
A limp shingle
He said, "A bat's
No business here"
And hammered it
Into the roof.

I laddered behind,
My hands tarred
With melt of shingles,
Trembling between
The bend of the staging—
And the lark of springing
Into the sky.

2. Sanding the Floor

Slowly, to and fro slowly, I spoil the varnish
and the half-moons—hobnail and spike—
pressed for a century to smeared prints
no one can read, or a soiled palm's lost lifeline.
Out of vain archeology, he rented this roller
to draw out the strata of wood, till

oak, tongue-in-groove, props me above
the dirt cellar, a palimpsest
which bleaches back to milky pulp—
pure and ready to print again.

3. Father Smoking

He builds for others,
but today in his green chair he reads
what he has no leisure for:

his lap book promises, floats
a stucco English cottage
with exploded views of every joist.

He daydreams cottage to palace,
then to the home
he had as a child among potato rows.

The roof sways in.
Walls open out like a vase,
and the cellar fills with peat until—

with blue rings he forms
the round, perfect tower
that keeps him building, climbing up.

4. The Cellar

Like an abandoned shop the room
below the kitchen silts with gloom.
Half-dug and paved only with soil,
its efforts die half spent: the oil
makes groan the white asbestos furnace
beside blurred dials of water and gas.

A quiet fort of craft: the wrench,
the level, and carpenter's bench,
a table set with vise and clamps,
where mice have tunnelled from the swamps
behind the panelled, detached doors,
and gypsy spiders tent the corners.

The door's small window fires a chute
of sun that sparks the dancing motes,
which loose and twist a double helix
that spins and climbs on wooden steps,
halfway to sun, and half from ground,
a dry and fecund start and end.

In musky smells of humid stone,
all wait the chance to rise again.

Self-Portrait as Bored Boy

A calm of cats-paws,
doldrums in the Seychelles.
The neck drops and fastens.
Vertebrae pause like iron
atop a granite plinth. The air
around vibrates mere space,
playing off the lead centre.
Nothing lures groundhog from its hole.
The coal-bed body lies stern
to the howls around it. This
graveyard of plans rests under
transparent snow. For hours he adores
a burnt match, stunned by an inner
whine and a thunder of pulse
that taps, taps. His shirt
is too heavy to unmove. Inside
a flashlight has dimmed, gone out.
No call for help. In a black hole
nothing bleats. For the time nothing
hurts, and fear grips like love.

The Quarrel

Hear them still:
father's silent
trap of smoke rings,
the snap and squish
of falling ash,
mother's loud arms
washing the moonlit walls,
my slipping into the hall,
cold stomach's
my rabbit thumping—

nightmare blaring
her shattering horn—

II

Everglades

I

Beneath Miami's honeycomb,
hurricanes clean Pa-Hay-Okee:
chloroplast sludge, a drain
where a heron selects a jack
and slash-pine is on the ascendant.
Tree-snails snatched,
collectors burn the copse.

II

Our night for Fire Ritual.
We claw each other.

In our anger you ask
love like an apoplectic child.

Cold and salt-tolerant as a shrew
I scout the lit Keys

over the patina of living
ooze not ten-feet deep.

Florida Bay never alters
like our shore, shifting

ancient fears and strikes,
fish we thought extinct.

Our feet crashing
the glassy mangrove leaves,

we each fancy the hackneyed
orange-peel moon,

the crass and lovely palmettos.

III

Our old trouble sleeps
in the crocodile-egg sun.
Our day, a hermit crab, crept
into the sun's blue shell.
We live the biology
of dead coral.

IV

A tree cranes its neck.
Wood stork?

We swing our fieldglasses.
White may flash a bird.

Alone and high,
we harden to tree-snails,

sway over the limestone
solution holes that boil,

hide above the perfect
'gator lair.

Our pine sways
its mast.

We mate. Then find real
snail eggs—relearn:

without fire,
hardwoods take over.

Studio Nude

Your contours design
a country refined
to curve and line.

The knotty serifs,
of bedclothes shift
the contours of floor and roof.

Only this cold crayon
graphs your motion,
arrays my mind.

English Fields

The wind snapping the ash trees,
our gray heron hidden in the rape,
the hare the tractor started,
the test pilots swooning over Kidlington:
once every quick and unmoving
parcel of landscape was tense.

Whose opinion peeped
from the tangled hedgerows—
an English mum's?—
as we followed the heron's tow-path trawling,
the fall raking his feathers?

What made us afraid? This
older country with our language?

The hare is gone. Fear migrates gently
like the heron's slow liftoff,
while the ash trees nod like benevolent nuns.

Familiar fears leave me naked.

Nocturne

You must, sir, love the abstract beauty
    of our muscular, hard faces
        who float summer pastels like moths
down littered streets, sell a galaxy
    of phantasma and spasmic graces
        beneath these tinder clothes.

And we must despise the desperation
    cruising your open cars,
        clown exhilaration
for you, and must always linger here
            in place of stars.

The Ascent of Snowdon

Thinking deeply of you and of distances without trees,
I climbed the spurs that rose sharp as mountains on old Japanese
lacquerware, the gray cracked paths that pared the sheep runs,
while a crew, like a chain gang, restacked the cast-down
homey walls, their hands hardly holding the broad stones
against dirty leather aprons and crooked knees.

Above, ceilings of peeled blue burned through
miniature fog clearings, short fast flights of sheep broke
in the uncurtaining penetralia of sun on the brink;
shale, brittler then, crushed to shattering arrowheads, clinked
my way uncertain, and a dizzying raven swooped a sharp hook.
My camera's eye failed. Fog-blind, I imagined you

lay by a city ocean and shielded your hand
against tidal-wave heat, frowning at children who swam
out and challenged lifeguards. You spoke with love
up to young men with curled hair to their shoulders
who stood and swayed on legs reddening to foxglove
beside slate-gray waves like distant moraine boulders.

The white wind then tore at my sweating frown
and wiped clean my bare shins and dry tongue. Like lost
divers, loving descenders loomed and tossed

in cottony air, mumbled luck, and passed down
towards the treasure troves of mountain pools
that blackened below in the cloud holes.

Then my black wool bleached to bright frosted hair
like yours, and my dark chest panted and sparked snowlight
beside real foxglove, that sheep hate, whose hung
red, sacrificed flowers flagged BELIEVE and swung
like a druid knife through caverns of wet air
at the rock's hard altars in the summit's night.

They Call It the "Wayfaring Tree"

(for Ann)

Unconstant viburnum barely held the hilltop,
pointing our house's northern corner, a gift
the month after we moved in—cold November.

Storm after storm, the tight green leaves twisted,
curled like children's fists against the drifts,
viburnum dragging its rangy new branches.

The givers parted. The taproot strikes deeper,
and the spring shrub renounces its name:
white blossoms for our hard staying on.

Forms in Contemporary Poetry

He was happy to throw it out,
the worn couch useless and hard
after the divorce. He knew
it might get taken, waiting
beside the hydrant in the snow
that fell harder, harder till
the couch turned marble,
without dignity or purpose,
something civic almost,
belonging to nothing else—
the reclining nude, like a hare's form gone.
That's how he thinks it.

A woman came, peered
through the snow. She
had it taken quickly and uncaked
the white before it vanished.
She knelt, as if in worship,
with sharp pins in her mouth,
measuring, then cutting.
A good tight fit,
and the braces stayed well.
So she uses it for sleep
and over and over for love.

In Bombay

At sunrise to pick over
the rubbish piles like gloves,
the crows come in black masks
and long grey dustcoats,
their whine as scheduled
as a neighbor's car.

Chief of the balcony rail,
one grunts for carrion.
His eyes swivel our bed.
He stares, bombastic and spruce
as any colonist,
a watchman on the wing for have.

I gun my fingers at
his game, nonviolent steps,
then swing the shutter to cage
out light. The district regained,
our restless breathing resumes—
barred shadows flutter across our eyes.

III

Changelings

This night from door
to door they beg,
like Odysseus in disguise
testing old hospitality.

They share the collective horror
which every fall laughs
death to a corn dolly
unhaying on the porch.

At my jack-o'-lantern, they pause.
"Trick or treat," chant the dead,
mimicking mischief, fidgeting
back to life with their "or else."

The majority claims its rights,
steps from dreams to notice,
and jokes for the sustenance to lurch
again out of our lives.

On Looking into Chapman

An acrid smell
fills him with the dust
of warm nettle.

He stalls by a window,
feels no rain
or thunder in the left meadow.

Unfavorably he sneezes,
and his crammed head pillows
on his Greek manual.

Till the evening
brings the field-crickets'
monotonous chirping.

Then the moon stops,
poised like a coin
in the mouth of a corpse.

—Twenty years ago he pines
below a hill near town.
Homer's horse neighs for him to climb.

He rises, hums a tune
heard in early childhood.
Homer paints a rune

upon his hand.—It revives.
Like a spider it cramps
across the tawny sheaves.

Lusty oil from his lamp
lights, not Troy Wall,
but Hitchin's alder swamp.

His stump of feather roughs
a path to the dark margin.
Like milking, the nib soughs.

Grayness unburies the northern sky.
A cart hobbles the track uphill.
He reads aloud. His words fall green and stony.

Cadres of critics fall in his fierce eye.

Knees

On seated statues' knees
ancients placed olive leaves.
On bent knee,
they begged mercy
from the conquerors,
saying, "I am yours,
a slave who reaches
for the winner's knees,
my own
unstrung."
A hinged joint
and target point
for a mobster's bullet
or a football hit.
Escape or weapon,
shuffle of religion's
involuntary reflex—
proposal or sex,
prop of force
for all fours.
With no such hocks,
a giant stalks
while frightened Belle stays,
and prays
with knee flexed
for flight,
for ruin and contest,
compassion, and caress.

Two Greek Sketchings

1. Donkeys

All over, and farther East, they crowd
shy stairways and nuzzle the shadows,
unready to undertake the brawny sun.

                                            Then heaving
us in wooden saddles like cradles,
all baled hair and wired muscle, they arch
us over their pommels, till we stiffen to centaurs, as
they dip and hold their eyes bland in the flinty wind.

To grapple their bony, chipped-out ledges,
they lower their necks in mock surrender, while
they bare their teeth, ears skewered up,
and throw us forward onto necks hard brown as dirt.

After we slide down, they re-caravan together,
congratulating in lithe gutturals,
muzzled bodies who wander nonchalant
from the gods who rode the crosses on their backs.

2. Greek Shadow Puppet

glad demon
swings longer arm
his modern

penis and flies
at bad Turk's eyes
with demotic cries

Byron's passion
this paper man
and the Indonesian's

nursery skit
through scrim sheet
secret treat

humped clown and sage
mocks his cage

unlocks all our rage

Paradise Lost

Sir Isaac Newton
Dreamed in his garden
Till an apple descended the tree.
Then wrote two volumes of sinful gravity.

Boustrophedon

> *"turning like oxen in ploughing; of writing*
> *from left to right and right to left alternately."*
> —Liddell and Scott, *A Greek-English Lexicon*

Near Gilbert White's house in Selbourne, Hants.,
,forest private almost his, Hangar the up follow you
the "Zig-Zag" he blazed early diagramming his certain
routine from way the of out turning non-orthodox but
sermons, small-town gossip, close family ties
,Spain criss-crossing birds of facta the into
or their hibernation—wrong, the academy had him there.
snow sweeping :flights own his had he Still
off his favorite trees, noting the flies cows kicked up,
hidden are and not really are that things ordinary the
though yeomen mocked such fruitless work.
:see now we direct was Zig-Zag White's
let others climb straight or list towards the right,
,zed the, omega his was path his for
the field his slow heart plowed completely.

Anecdote of a Novelist

She declines her head
till half-mooned by the lamp.

It is her August party,
and everything she drew

from the housefuls of artists
who stood in her father's drawing room

is displayed tonight, though the wit
now is decidedly anti-Victorian:

less is better. Yet no one
will take away enough of her "arrangements,"

told in her sharp, brittle way.
The lamp bulb labors

under the green Tiffany,
as she labors, to please.

When she completes her
impromptu truths,

she appoints a girl of eighteen
in a corner as her last

lift: "Now *you* tell
us something clever—won't you?"

The crowd stirs at first
less glad, then laughter

sways them, as chestnuts
sway their heavy summer candles.

The girl chirps nothing, sinks
through the rest. Till,

rising for home, she feels
a hit swell in the bruise:

"'But *I* have not prepared
anything, my dear.'

Think what would happen
if I said that.

Think of the chestnut
swaying its leaves."

Jungle Boy: Folk Artist

(Bynum, NC)

The Haw River Mill closed
and he went mad, hauled
home the virgin timber
whose pine eyes cursed him before
in the sliced wood, creatures
who crossed his future.
So he cut devils with a chain saw,
muzzles and owl ears sprung
from the fairytale wood,
and whittled giraffe necks,
pangolin snouts, 'gator jaws, that stared
with real light bulbs and tennis balls.

—And stare still, like wild piñatas,
in Carolina's shade-deep yards.

Coal Mine Museum

Before each snapshot, we stare briefly
at the blackened faces as if we *could*
hear them cough black damp, while their wives,
camera-shy, hang out stained clothes—
we've seen such black-and-whites before.

Shadow everywhere: the coal breaker
looms like a royal barn on stilts,
more than black fills the shafts
beyond our adit. "Deep in the Bone
of Earth," they'd sing—but we know

these Polish names are dead. On some
the wick breathed blue for twenty seconds more.
Others lost to oil the art of delving,
spotting the petrified elm leaf, busting
the battery for the glint to funnel like hail.

Picture them Cyclops-eyed and Indian-file, swinging
candles in glass, returning into this cut,
like a snake—

                But we stand on tour,
the one moving thing a bat
our guide enrages with a shaft of light.

Chinese Gallery

These paintings don't show dragons,
or snarling guardian spirits or Foo Dogs—
just miniatures in dark robes,
a third of the way up a mountain,
climbing past carefully composed pagodas,
teahouses, and foot-bridged ponds.
Even birds are scant. Calligraphy
in the margin comments on the quality
of the art, but tells us nothing
really, like why they seem
always to go up, never down,
and more importantly how part
of the landscape is mere air that
we must fill in. Perhaps
those white spaces are ours
to see the drift into
eternity that the present
always provides, never filling
in the whole space, unlike children,
who color all sky and yard and house,
putting it together like a puzzle.
Surely here part of the puzzle is
lost, or is part of something else.

But what is missed stays here
in what may be snow: that

path to the fourth dimension:
the city and the network of
friends and enemies who have been
taken out, who do not lead to this
cold elevation of self, where only
the priest and the novice are
always on the ascendant, leaving
things out of the world, finding
not things, but the negative forms
of things and color patches like footprints,
whitening out, as it were, objects,
till only a few landmarks are left,
but just enough, so that they—and we—
can find the way back again through
the vanishing ground and the words in the margin
that mark the way.

IV

Wolf Howl

Before the blackout, our cordon
of headlights jammed seven miles.
Beyond are the wolves, though
no one sees them but winter rangers
airlifting endangered moose
over snow to thicker woods.
But the wolves wander at will.

In summer we trick them to entertain
us, who rarely see beaver,
whose children are slumped and dreaming.
We stroll tamely, hushed
on the edge of the greater dark,
hoping for the miracle.

                         The rangers
lob three long calls that dive
in blackness, then
                             instinct yammers.
A chaotic band tunes: yelps,
tired wails, lift and mix,
crescendo to harmony—hover—
and die, like a Roman candle.

The next hoax loses ground.
Only the young still believe we threaten

the land: occasional yawping, till—
our rangers go unanswered.
The dark closes to an empty theatre.

Our caravan decamps, lights up
the one road. Keeping radios
at bay, we wagon-train to
our motels,
            satisfied,
                      elated.

Fern

They loll and talk past-glory.
In shade when the wind stirs they bury
vague flags. Their heads blur
and swing on the silted forest floor.

A flurry accepts their smallness,
the hundred feet or more lost
with the power to break down wind
or bend long shafts of sun.

If the forest repeats, they happily
would devour dwarfing red maple,
less hateful of the tall greenness
a clumsy forest spills once.

Sailing to the Isle of Man

In the sordid ship
exhausted commuters sleep,
approach through golden gauze,
confess, "It isn't on this water."

Beneath the copper sun
boys chase the corridors
above the fuming oil,
verify, "This is no time for planning."

The bald headland answers,
"A mist bragged your island
where Vikings would casually founder,
a heron pilfer the shadows."

Climber

A bald head rises
on Wright's Wilderness Tower.

Shouldering his love of challenged stone,
he boots hard on my platform of slate.

"Nature's way is up and down," he jokes.
Scorner of the last snow rivulets

running off to the sink-hole sea,
annihilator of solar mantras,

he glances neither east nor west.
But scales straightdown the present blue.

His grip firm on the red braid.
His eyes cold as the day-moon.

Caribou

Mutual wounds are mended—
the scarrings of fierce marriages.

In blue-black winter days,
    they shed and eat their antlers,
        nestle, like huskies, in snow,

till tundra stirs gray water
    and they take stock of their remaining herd.

Even then their path is twisted
    by permafrost forest
        tilting trees each way
            like a drunken army's guns.

One buck demands the headland.
    When he breaks, all stampede,
        brown patches and winter white—

a landscape falling to pieces—
    and, restless as auroras, they crest
        streams, like sweeper trees,
            knees aquiver with wolves

till screened in grass, they maneuver
    rest, twitching deerflies.
        Or unmoving by glacial erratics,
            tailspin to a bullet.

In green, in white spaces,
    they guard our magnetic north,

then walk on water,
    locked in the river like bone,
        to the dying campfire of horizon

promising another sun.

Icework

Like a hack turned out of harness
after ice-cutting days, my lab
sludges the silver path the moon polishes
beside the ice-house memorial and vanished winches.

I follow her retriever shamble
and flatten my feet on packed snow to balance
—then her leash leaps my hand and she bolts
over the pond bank, swims the dense air

sniffing, scraping the drum-tight edge of boilerplate ice.
A throb and sway in the polar light,
she points with lifelines of memory and crouches
in a wild yawn, alive to each branch snap.

She's caught the ice groan and awaits
further calving, born in new shafts splitting down.
She backs from the black water's rigor mortis,
as if to yield room, whimpering anticipation.

Then low thunder. And she sports side to side,
twists and bows, yelps to wake the dead.
Her lonely mind answers the pond's deep bark—
where a trapped cutter kicked and coughed.

Firework

Still we must look at the exploding patterns
falling over us like wicked fingers of fire
playing impromptu upon the dark keys
with deft uncontrol: these can't make faces
like campfires, or straighten like match spurts,
are reminiscent barely of Japanese chrysanthemums
or Roman Catholic candles blistering up over
congregations or willows crying paper sparks.
Relays of small explosions follow—codas
puncturing the dim air with confetti light.
Till a finale spawns a vase of rocketshells,
red, orange, yellow, clawing to stay in the black.
Then a final whizz-bang. And the pause, where some darkness
says, "Is it over?" And the slow fuse of talk reignites.

Rehearsal: *Eclipse of the Sun*

The hidden moon appears—a head
that blocks the brassy sun,
like a tall man cutting off your book
from a halogen lamp.

But the moon haloes with a ring
of Arctic light, and rounds
with such fire, you must
avert your eyes.

It has gained theatre depths,
bordered by a husk of procreation,
a dead player, backlit, in the noon-night—
till the moon passes.

Now glimpse the dark disk
fall back into the sky through the forced light,
which kills centuries of angels and ash,
the earth relit from its kiss.

Desert Ruins

You might take the mesquite for caravans
and its raven for a black flag.
The gravel fans could be fallen
gardens in an unsettled mind.

Still there is such emptiness
a desert must be crumbled and reborn.
Rebuilding proceeds apace: the moon
does odd jobs and the coyote yowl.

The day color of mountains is wash
when one plane reshapes another,
and slim shadows help
the cactus fingers *V* good luck.

Your eerie city won't spoil
the crust of the hills.
Once the salt pan is peopled,
the only necessity is to keep castling.

Afloat in Dogtown Moraine

"I paint rocks & rocks only."
—Marsden Hartley at Dogtown, Mass.

Some are fat as a small ship,
and have a tree split
through the middle for a mast.
All sank in the mass
of ice and the mud and stone
from flayed ground,
till it was a river of rock,
alive with gull talk,
wind spill, and the churn
of a brook. Beech arms
swim in the rocky froth,
and the clouds float
in blue, like icebergs, as above
the ill painter who solved
their dictation, though
the rocks were endowed
with slogans rigidly engraved:
IDEAS and WORK and SAVE.
America's hard glory,
that made him sit and dally
in this rocky fen,
attentive to the fluid stone.

The other who carved the rocks
knew he would not be back,

made his "last and permanent
protest" against the collapsed settlement
and the ineffable boulders
dropped by the ice before
it backtracked. The moraine
was a gift that would remain.
On it he cut his platitudes:
BE ON TIME, GET A JOB, STUDY,
HELP MOTHER, KINDNESS, TRUTH,
comic-book morality, we trust,
who cannot see their application.
"Relativistic empiricism,"
he would have countered,
who penned his books outdoors
and who was abashed
that promiscuous plants flourished.
"Roger, you are ruining our rocks,"
Mrs. Babson complained. "Sacrilege,"
thought Hartley the painter. But
it was on *his* land that
he shaped messages to sky,
converting the rocks to high
language, just as the overgrown cellar frames
had to be given historical names,
because he could not be here and not
have some grand word for it.

The force that dropped the boulders
trapped the settlers

among the rocky arks
and shadowed booths and the black
flaking deer lichen.
These rocky facets do not strike
points of light, and one hides
a black silhouette inside:
a boy seated on the ground,
his brow raised to heaven.
Only a desert father could help
him out of these heaps,
an accident of rocky gloss
that marks one who has lost
mother, and father's voice
holds like the granite ice—
until I apportion with my eye
and cut a rune sententiously.
Then my shadow lifts free.

Notes

Bells off Salvador
matanza: massacre. *los desaparecidos*: the "disappeared," missing persons. San Juan de la Cruz: Saint John of the Cross.

First Step at Scilla
Scilla is a town in Southern Italy, the Scylla of myth.

On Looking into Chapman
George Chapman was a mystic as well as the Renaissance translator of Homer.

Anecdote of a Novelist
Based on an anecdote about Virginia Woolf, told by Nigel Nicolson in a lecture at Oxford.

Afloat in Dogtown Moraine
Dogtown is an old, ruined village on Cape Ann, Massachusetts. Marsden Hartley painted a series of paintings there. It is also a glacial moraine, upon whose rocks Roger Babson, the founder of Babson College, had moral slogans carved.

A Note on the Author

Francis Blessington is a literary critic and a translator as well as a poet. He is a professor of English at Northeastern University. He lives in Woburn, Massachusetts, with his wife, essayist Ann Taylor, and their two children, Geoffrey and Julia.